AR Quiz # 157141
BL: 4.8   AR PTS: 0.5

EXPLORING COUNTRIES
New Zealand

by Ellen Frazel

BLASTOFF!
5
READERS

BELLWETHER MEDIA · MINNEAPOLIS, MN

Note to Librarians, Teachers, and Parents:

Blastoff! Readers are carefully developed by literacy experts and combine standards-based content with developmentally appropriate text.

Level 1 provides the most support through repetition of high-frequency words, light text, predictable sentence patterns, and strong visual support.

Level 2 offers early readers a bit more challenge through varied simple sentences, increased text load, and less repetition of high-frequency words.

Level 3 advances early-fluent readers toward fluency through increased text and concept load, less reliance on visuals, longer sentences, and more literary language.

Level 4 builds reading stamina by providing more text per page, increased use of punctuation, greater variation in sentence patterns, and increasingly challenging vocabulary.

Level 5 encourages children to move from "learning to read" to "reading to learn" by providing even more text, varied writing styles, and less familiar topics.

Whichever book is right for your reader, Blastoff! Readers are the perfect books to build confidence and encourage a love of reading that will last a lifetime!

This edition first published in 2013 by Bellwether Media, Inc.

No part of this publication may be reproduced in whole or in part without written permission of the publisher. For information regarding permission, write to Bellwether Media, Inc., Attention: Permissions Department, 5357 Penn Avenue South, Minneapolis, MN 55419.

Library of Congress Cataloging-in-Publication Data
Frazel, Ellen.
New Zealand / by Ellen Frazel.
    p. cm. – (Blastoff! readers: Exploring countries)
Includes bibliographical references and index.
Summary: "Developed by literacy experts for students in grades three through seven, this book introduces young readers to the geography and culture of New Zealand"–Provided by publisher.
ISBN 978-1-60014-862-0 (hardcover : alk. paper)
1. New Zealand–Juvenile literature. I. Title.
DU408.F73 2013
993–dc23

2012033444

Contents

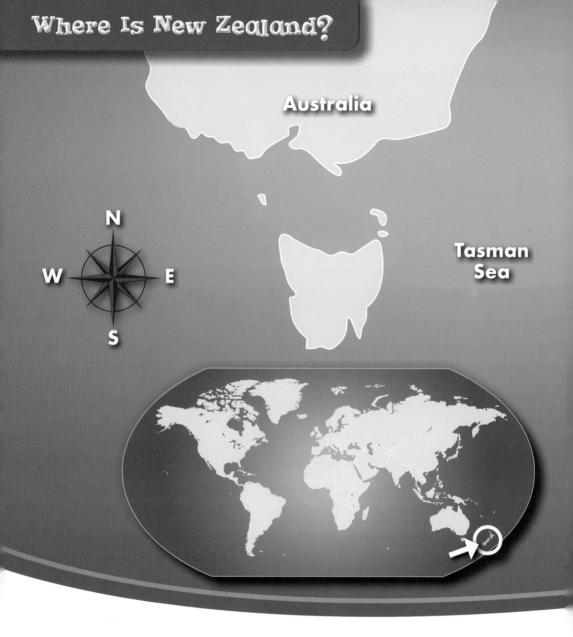

New Zealand is an island country in the southwest Pacific Ocean. It lies more than 1,000 miles (1,600 kilometers) southeast of Australia across the Tasman Sea. Its other closest neighbors are the island countries of New Caledonia, Fiji, and Tonga. They are about 600 miles (1,000 kilometers) north in the Pacific Ocean.

New Zealand

Cook Strait

★ **Wellington**

Pacific Ocean

! fun fact
Wellington is the southernmost capital in the world.

New Zealand covers a total of 103,363 square miles (267,710 square kilometers). Its two main landmasses are the North and South Islands. These islands are separated by the Cook **Strait**. New Zealand's capital, Wellington, sits on the southern tip of the North Island.

Mount Cook

New Zealand's largest island is the South Island. The Southern Alps rise along its length. Icy **glaciers** cover mountain slopes that tower above forests. The glaciers feed sparkling rivers and lakes in the valleys below. In the southwestern corner, deep **fjords** cut into steep mountains.

! **fun fact**

Tasman Glacier in the Southern Alps is New Zealand's longest glacier. It stretches 18 miles (29 kilometers) down Mount Cook, the country's tallest peak.

The North Island features the Volcanic **Plateau** at its center. Three active **volcanoes** dot this region. One of them is Mount Ruapehu, the North Island's highest mountain.

The Taupo Volcanic Zone on the North Island of New Zealand formed hundreds of thousands of years ago. Movement of Earth's crust created large volcanoes there. They stretch in a V shape for about 220 miles (350 kilometers).

The volcanic zone is named after the beautiful Lake Taupo. Covering 234 square miles (606 square kilometers), it is the largest lake in New Zealand. It fills a **caldera** created by a violent volcanic eruption about 26,500 years ago. Today people take in the view of distant volcanoes as they swim, water-ski, and sail in Lake Taupo's blue-green waters.

fun fact

The Craters of the Moon is a popular destination near Lake Taupo. Visitors walk among clouds of steam and boiling mud pools in this valley of craters.

Craters of the Moon

Lake Taupo

kea

New Zealand's only **native** land mammals are two **species** of bats. The long-tailed bat comes out at night to snatch bugs from the air. The rare short-tailed bat searches for insects and fruit along the forest floor. Crawling nearby are tuataras and weta, two animals that were also on the island before it was settled.

10

tuataras

weta

kiwi

fun fact
New Zealanders are nicknamed "kiwis" after the flightless kiwi. This native bird is a national symbol of New Zealand.

Fantails, kea, and other native birds make their homes in the country's forests. Penguins waddle along the coasts while albatrosses and petrels fly over the water. Fur seals live in colonies on the coasts of the South Island and lower North Island. Dolphins and whales swim in the waters off the coast.

Maori

Over 4 million people live in New Zealand. More than half of them are European. Their **ancestors** came from Great Britain, Ireland, and other parts of Europe. People from China, South Korea, and other Asian countries make up another large group.

The first people to settle New Zealand were the Maori. They came from Eastern **Polynesia** about 1,000 years ago. Today, the Maori are a significant people group. English and Maori are the country's two official languages.

Speak Maori!

English	Maori	How to say it
hello	tēnā koe	tay-NAH-kway
good-bye	e noho rā	ay-no-ho-RAH
yes	āe	eye
no	kāore	KAH-oh-ray
please	koa	kwah
thank you	kia ora	kee-ah-AW-rah
friend	hoa	hwah

Daily Life

Most New Zealanders live in cities on the North Island. Coastal cities like Wellington and Auckland feature houses overlooking beautiful beaches and blue waters. Many people make their homes in apartments or houses farther from the coast. They take trains, cable cars, and buses to work or school.

People also live in **suburbs** and on farms in the countryside. They take trains or drive cars into the city to work or visit friends. Many New Zealanders take a **ferry** to the South Island or fly to nearby Australia for vacation.

Where People Live in New Zealand

countryside
14%

cities
86%

Auckland

Did you know?

Auckland is known as the "City of Sails." Boats of all sizes decorate its shoreline. About one in three families in Auckland owns a boat.

School in New Zealand is required from ages 5 to 16. Primary school lasts eight years. Students learn basic math, writing, reading, and science. Some schools offer classes in the Maori language. In secondary school, students study literature and other more advanced subjects.

Students can attend university after secondary school. They earn a bachelor's degree after three years. Students usually stay for a fourth year to complete their education with an honors degree.

Where People Work in New Zealand

manufacturing 19%

services 74%

farming 7%

Did you know?

With over 6 million dairy cattle in the country, New Zealand is the eighth largest milk producer in the world.

Most New Zealanders have **service jobs**.
They work in banks, hospitals, and other places
that help people. Many New Zealanders serve
the country's **tourists**. They run hotels, host
nature tours, and show visitors the sights.

Some people in New Zealand work in factories.
They make wood products, **textiles**, and
transportation equipment. In the countryside,
farmers raise sheep for their meat and wool.
They also grow wheat, barley, and other crops.
Some New Zealanders make their living fishing
off the coast for shellfish and other seafood.

zorbing

New Zealanders have a passion for outdoor adventures. Bungee jumping and **zorbing** are extreme sports that were invented in the country. People also enjoy hiking, canoeing, and other recreational activities that allow them to experience New Zealand's natural beauty.

Competitive sports are also popular. New Zealanders especially love to play and watch rugby, a sport similar to American football. Cricket and netball are other favorites. Cricket is played with a ball and bat on an oval field. Netball is a version of basketball.

! fun fact

Skydiving is another extreme sport that gets the heart pumping in New Zealand. People can skydive over Lake Taupo and other stunning landscapes in the country.

hangi

Food in New Zealand is influenced by the different peoples of the country. Dishes have flavors from Europe, Asia, Polynesia, and other regions. For breakfast, people typically eat something simple like porridge, cereal, or eggs. Coffee or tea is served alongside. Lunch may be the famous English fish and chips. Oysters, mussels, and other shellfish are served at restaurants and waterside cafés.

Roasted lamb is a favorite dinner in New Zealand. A sweet potato called kumara is often roasted as a side dish. A traditional Maori dinner is a stew called boil-up. This includes pork, kumara, leafy greens, and potatoes. *Pavlova* is the national dessert of New Zealand. This is a light cake topped with whipped cream and fresh fruit.

! fun fact

Pavlova is named after the Russian ballerina Anna Pavlova. It is light and airy like a graceful dancer.

pavlova

kumara

kumara in *hangi*

Many New Zealanders celebrate Christian holidays.
Christmas takes place in the summertime in New Zealand.
Families throw barbeques and relax at the beach.
Easter occurs in the fall. As leaves fall from the trees,
New Zealanders still enjoy springtime decorations and
Easter egg hunts.

Did you know?
On Waitangi Day, some Maori dress in traditional clothing and paddle wakas, or war canoes.

Holidays that mark events in New Zealand's history are also celebrated. February 6 is Waitangi Day. New Zealand was officially founded on this day in 1840. Major cities hold festivals and ceremonies on Waitangi Day. April 25 is Anzac Day. This holiday honors all New Zealanders who have died fighting for the country. People parade in the streets and wear red poppies as a symbol of remembrance.

The Maori are believed to have traveled from Eastern Polynesia to New Zealand around 1000 CE. They were **astronomers** skilled at traveling long distances across the ocean. When Europeans settled in New Zealand centuries later, the Maori became the smaller group. However, their distinct traditions have become central to the island's culture over the years.

Maori New Year, or *Matariki*, is now celebrated throughout the country. It occurs in late May or early June when a group of stars called the **Pleiades** rises. Traditionally, this was a time for the Maori to prepare for the next year after harvesting their crops. Today people celebrate with art festivals, concerts, and kite flying. By honoring this day and celebrating other Maori traditions, New Zealanders connect their country's rich past to its vibrant present.

Did you know?
In addition to flying kites, New Zealanders launch hot air balloons and light fireworks on *Matariki*. These celebrations bring them closer to the stars!

Fast Facts About New Zealand

New Zealand's Flag

The flag of New Zealand is blue with the flag of the United Kingdom in the upper left corner. This flag, called the Union Jack, represents the time when the British settled New Zealand. Centered in the right half of the flag are four red stars. They symbolize the Southern Cross, a group of stars that shines bright above New Zealand.

Official Name: New Zealand

Area: 103,363 square miles (267,710 square kilometers); New Zealand is the 76th largest country in the world.

Capital City:	Wellington
Important Cities:	Auckland, Christchurch, Hamilton
Population:	4,327,944 (July 2012)
Official Languages:	English, Maori
National Holiday:	Waitangi Day (February 6)
Religions:	Christian (51.2%), None (32.2%), Other (12.1%), Maori Christian (1.6%), Hindu (1.6%), Buddhist (1.3%)
Major Industries:	dairy farming, fishing, mining, services, tourism
Natural Resources:	lumber, coal, iron, gold, limestone, hydropower
Manufactured Products:	wood and paper products, textiles, transportation equipment
Farm Products:	wheat, barley, potatoes, kiwis, wool, dairy products, lamb, beef, fish
Unit of Money:	New Zealand dollar; the New Zealand dollar is divided into 100 cents.

Glossary

ancestors—relatives who lived long ago

astronomers—scientists who study the stars, planets, and galaxies; the Maori were astronomers who used the stars as guides during ocean travel.

caldera—a giant crater that is formed when a volcano collapses after an eruption

ferry—a boat or ship used to carry passengers across a body of water

fjords—long, narrow inlets of the ocean between tall cliffs; the movement of glaciers makes fjords.

glaciers—massive sheets of ice that cover a large area of land

native—originally from a specific place

plateau—an area of flat, raised land

Pleiades—a cluster of very bright stars; the Pleiades is one of the closest star clusters to Earth and one of the easiest to see with the naked eye.

Polynesia—a region in the South Pacific Ocean made up of hundreds of islands

service jobs—jobs that perform tasks for people or businesses

species—groups of related animals; all animals in a species have the same characteristics.

strait—a narrow stretch of water that connects two larger bodies of water

suburbs—communities that lie just outside a city

textiles—fabrics or clothes that have been woven or knitted

tourists—people who travel to visit another country

volcanoes—holes in the earth; when a volcano erupts, hot, melted rock called lava shoots out.

zorbing—the extreme sport of rolling down a hill inside a large ball made of clear plastic

To Learn More

AT THE LIBRARY

Colson, Mary. *New Zealand*. Chicago, Ill.: Heinemann Library, 2012.

Larson, Lyn. *New Zealand*. Minneapolis, Minn.: Lerner Publications, 2011.

Theunissen, Steve. *The Maori of New Zealand*. Minneapolis, Minn.: Lerner Publications, 2003.

ON THE WEB

Learning more about New Zealand is as easy as 1, 2, 3.

1. Go to www.factsurfer.com.

2. Enter "New Zealand" into the search box.

3. Click the "Surf" button and you will see a list of related Web sites.

With factsurfer.com, finding more information is just a click away.

Index

The images in this book are reproduced through the courtesy of: Martin Maun, front cover; Pichugin Dmitry, pp. 6-7; Rafael Ben-Ari/Chameleons Eye/Newscom, p. 8; Age Fotostock/SuperStock, p. 9; Simon Larkin, pp. 10-11; Cameramannz, p. 10 (top); Graham Prentice, p. 10 (middle); Steve Vidler/SuperStock, pp. 10 (bottom), 12; Tim Graham/Getty Images, p. 14 (small); Andrew Lever, pp. 14-15; Cusp/SuperStock, pp. 16-17; Zambezishark, p. 18; Bloomberg/Getty Images, p. 19 (left); Colin Monteath/Age Fotostock/SuperStock, p. 19 (right); Macsnap, p. 20; R. Ian Lloyd/Masterfile, p. 21; Paul Almasy/Corbis, p. 22; ElenaGaak, p. 23 (top); eye-blink, p. 23 (middle); Nic Neish, p. 23 (bottom); Associated Press, pp. 24-25; travelstock44/Getty Images, p. 26; Daiviet, p. 27; Jennifer Gottschalk, p. 29.